QUESTIONING HISTORY

The Arab-Israeli Conflict

Cath Senker

HODDER
Wayland

an imprint of Hodder Children's Books

© 2004 White-Thomson Publishing Ltd

Produced for Hodder Wayland by
White-Thomson Publishing Ltd
2/3 St Andrew's Place
Lewes BN7 1UP

Other titles in this series:
The African-American Slave Trade
The American West
The Causes of World War II
The Cold War
The French Revolution
The Holocaust
Nazi Germany
The Western Front

Editor: Kelly Davis
Designer: Jamie Asher
Consultant: Avi Shlaim
Picture researcher: Kelly Davis
Proofreader: David C. Sills, Proof Positive
Reading Service

Published in Great Britain in 2004 by Hodder
Wayland, an imprint of Hodder Children's Books

The right of Cath Senker to be identified as the
author has been asserted by her in accordance with
the Copyright, Designs and Patents Act 1988.

British Library Cataloguing in Publication Data
Senker, Cath
  The Arab-Israeli Conflict.- (Questioning
  History) 1. Arab Israeli conflict - Juvenile
  literature I. Title
  956.9'405
  ISBN 0 7502 4516 6

Printed by C&C Offset Printing Co., Ltd. China

Hodder Children's Books
A division of Hodder Headline Limited
338 Euston Road, London NW1 3BH

Picture acknowledgements:

Corbis 10 (Minnesota Historical Society), 19, 21
and 45 (Bettmann), 36 (Sobi); Hodder Wayland
Picture Library 18, 20, 33, 37, 42 (Mounir Nasr),
60, 61; Popperfoto 5 (Rula Halawani), 6 and 55
(Havakuk Levison), 8 and *cover* (Mahfouz Abu
Turk), 9 (Reinhard Krause), 11, 12, 14/15, 16, 17,
23, 25, 26, 27, 28, 29, 30, 31, 34 and *title page*, 38
(Yossi Roth), 39 (Walter Wisniewski), 40
(M. Gangne), 41, 43 (Suhaib Salem), 46, 47, 48
(Esaias Baitel), 49 (M. Nelson), 50, 51, 52, 53, 54,
56 (Evelyn Hockstein), 57 (Nayef Hashlamoun),
59 (Hussein Malla).

The maps on pages 4, 32 and 35 were produced
by The Map Studio. The map on p. 32 is adapted
from a map in *Righteous Victims* by Benny Morris
(Vintage Books, 2001), p. 293. The map on p. 35
is adapted from a map in *Righteous Victims*, p. 315.

Cover picture: An Israeli soldier gestures towards
Palestinians at Kalandia checkpoint as they enter
Ramallah, West Bank, during a temporary lifting of
the curfew, July 2002.

CONTENTS

CHAPTER 1

A Continuing Conflict

In its short life, Israel has built a modern state, with highly developed industries and agriculture. Its 6 million inhabitants are mostly Jewish people, originating from many different countries. About 1 million are Palestinian Arabs.

Around 3 million Palestinian Arabs live in the West Bank, Gaza Strip and East Jerusalem, generally called the Occupied Territories. The Palestinian Authority (established in 1993) runs local affairs but does not rule an independent state. The Israeli army controls these territories using force and the Palestinians resist the occupation using force. Peace negotiations between Israel and the Palestinians have repeatedly stalled.

BELOW *A map showing the territory of Israel (white) and Palestinian territory occupied by Israel (shaded areas).*

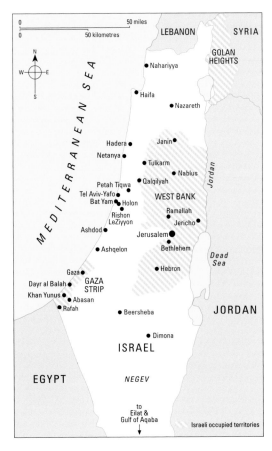

ISRAEL AND ITS ARAB NEIGHBOURS

Since its formation in 1948, Israel and the Arab states have been enemies. Israel was established through war (see page 28). During that conflict, over half of the Palestinian people were forced to leave their homes. Some moved to the West Bank and Gaza Strip as refugees, while many sought refuge in the neighbouring Arab countries of Lebanon, Syria and Jordan. The rulers of the Arab countries were unhappy about accommodating the refugees.

There have been regular international efforts to promote peace agreements in order to secure borders and prevent aggression between the countries. In 2003, there was an uneasy peace between Israel and its neighbours, Egypt and Jordan, but no agreement with Syria or Lebanon had been achieved.

ABOVE *An Israeli border-police patrol passing an elderly Palestinian beggar on the way into the Arab Old City of Jerusalem, 1997.*

The international community has an interest in achieving stability in the Middle East. However, throughout the region, most Arab people live under corrupt and deeply unpopular governments. The Middle East remains a tinderbox that could easily ignite into greater conflict than has yet been seen. Ending conflict in the region would involve bringing justice to the Palestinians without damaging Israel. It would also mean resolving the differences between Israel and its Arab neighbours, and between Arab governments and their people.

? EVENT IN QUESTION

The expulsion of the Palestinians from Israel, 1947–9

The expulsion of 750,000 Palestinians in the 1947–9 war is the basis of the Israeli-Palestinian conflict. The refugees were never allowed to return. Some Israelis argue that the Palestinians should receive help from the Arab states rather than from Israel, a Jewish country. As fellow Arabs, they could easily absorb them into their countries and they would not need to continue living as refugees. The Palestinians, however, argue that they have the right to return to their land.

ISRAELI INSECURITY

Israel is a vibrant, modern society, known for its sophisticated culture and world-class academic institutions, but living with constant conflict takes its toll. Israelis feel insecure because the neighbouring countries are hostile to them. They can visit Egypt and Jordan but Syria, Lebanon and most other Arab countries are out of bounds. The army forms a vital part of Israeli society. Everyone, with few exceptions, has to do army service – men for three years and most women for two years. There is also the ever-present fear of terrorist attack. Many Israelis have lost family members in bombings and shootings.

Political insecurity causes economic insecurity. Because of the Al-Aqsa intifada (see page 50), Israel has had to spend more on the military and on welfare, leading to a decline in economic growth. The USA has always supported Israel, giving it more

BELOW *The Jewish settlement of Kfar Oranim in the West Bank, near the Palestinian village of Safa (seen in the background), 1997. Settlers said they moved there because they wanted a comfortable suburban lifestyle.*

economic and military aid than any other country. The Israeli economy is totally dependent on US aid, receiving $3 billion to $5 billion each year.

A DIVIDED SOCIETY

There are divisions within Israeli society. For example, most Israelis live within the borders established after the 1967 war (see page 35). But there are nearly 200,000 Jewish settlers living in the Israeli-occupied West Bank and Gaza Strip, and about 180,000 living in East Jerusalem. Many have moved there because housing is cheaper. A significant minority live there because they believe that the whole area, from the Mediterranean Sea to the River Jordan, forms the Land of Israel, given to them by God. However, around half of Israelis believe that Israel should give up most of the settlements in exchange for peace.

The Palestinian Arabs within Israel feel they are treated as second-class citizens. For example, 100 Arab villages are not officially recognized, so they get few services, despite paying their taxes. Arab children are educated separately and their schools receive less funding than those attended by Jewish-Israeli children. Although Arabs have the vote, their political parties have always been left out of Israeli governments.

? PEOPLE IN QUESTION

Azmi Al-Bishara

Azmi Al-Bishara (b. 1956) is one of only nine Arabs in the 120-member Knesset, the Israeli parliament. In December 2002, his party, the National Democratic Assembly, was banned from participating in the elections the following month. Al-Bishara was accused, among other things, of *'denying the existence of Israel as a Jewish and a democratic state'*. He claimed there was a *'built-in contradiction between a Jewish state on the one hand, and a democratic state on the other. Such a contradiction can only be resolved through a state for all its citizens.'* Is Al-Bishara right? Or should Israel, the only Jewish state in the world, remain so?

Daily Life for Palestinians

Since the Palestinians renewed their struggle to win an independent state from Israel in September 2000 (see page 50), things have got tougher. By July 2003, over 2,400 Palestinians had been killed and more than 23,000 injured. Israel has used collective punishment to try to stop the resistance – punishing a whole community if it is believed that some of its members have attacked Israelis. ('If they [the Palestinians] aren't badly beaten, there won't be any negotiations,' said Ariel Sharon, Israeli Prime Minister, in 2002.) Checkpoints and roadblocks divide the West Bank into 300 separate clusters, and the Gaza Strip into three clusters, so towns and cities can be cut off at will.

The Palestinian economy is in tatters. Most Palestinians are refugees, living in tiny, cramped shacks, and about half the Palestinian workforce is unemployed. A shocking 70 per cent of Palestinians in Gaza, and 55 per cent in the West Bank, live below the poverty line, surviving on less than US$2 a day.

BELOW An Israeli soldier gestures towards Palestinians at Kalandia checkpoint as they enter Ramallah, West Bank, during a temporary lifting of the curfew, July 2002. As well as making people's lives difficult, curfews cause terrible damage to the Palestinian economy.

A FRACTURED SOCIETY

Some Palestinians feel that the best way forward is to negotiate with Israel to achieve independence, while others believe that it is necessary to fight. Of these, some groups, such as Hamas and Islamic Jihad, want an Islamic state in Palestine, and they present a challenge to the Palestinian Authority, which does not support this aim. The unrelenting, bitter conflict means that it is very hard for democracy to develop under the Palestinian Authority.

ABOVE *A Palestinian man gives bread to a boy in the remains of their destroyed home in Jenin refugee camp, West Bank, April 2002.*

? EVENT IN QUESTION

'Operation Defensive Wall', April 2002

In early 2002 a series of suicide bombings took place. Palestinians wearing explosives went to crowded areas in Israel, blowing themselves up and killing and maiming Israeli citizens. Over 100 Israelis lost their lives. In response, Israeli Prime Minister Ariel Sharon ordered Operation Defensive Wall to attack Palestinian cities in the West Bank. Schools, offices and clinics were shelled. Over 6,000 Palestinians were arrested. Nearly 17,000 Palestinians had their homes demolished. In Jenin, at least 52 Palestinians were killed. The aim was to target the terrorists who had committed atrocities in Israel. Was the Israeli army's action justifiable, in order to deter future terrorists? Or was this a crime against Palestinian civilians?

CHAPTER 2

What are the Origins of the Conflict?

In the 1880s, 90 per cent of the world's Jewish population lived in Europe and Russia. The Jews of Romania, Austria-Hungary and Russia suffered from terrible poverty and persecution. Russia was ruled by a Tsar who appointed his own government. Most Russians farmed the land as serfs, working for wealthy landowners. They wanted to own their land and have some freedom.

BELOW *Polish and Russian people travelling to America by ship in the early 1900s. Conditions on the journey were often harsh but Jewish emigrants were prepared to put up with the hardship for the chance of a life free of fear.*

BLAMING THE JEWS

Most Jewish people also lived in the countryside, working as tradespeople, farmers and rent collectors. The Tsar's government grew more unpopular in the late nineteenth century and Jews were blamed for the problems in society. As a separate group, with their own religion and customs, it was easy to pick on them.

The government encouraged this, passing laws against the Jews. Ordinary people then took the law into their own hands, killing and injuring thousands of Jews in vicious attacks known as pogroms.

Meanwhile, in western Europe, the nineteenth century also saw the rise of anti-Semitism – prejudice against the Jews. Even though they had previously been treated as equal citizens, there was now a widespread feeling in countries such as France, Austria and Germany that Jewish people were unwelcome outsiders.

ANTI-SEMITISM AND THE BIRTH OF ZIONISM

In Russia, some Jewish people firmly believed that Russians were not naturally anti-Semitic but were being encouraged to attack the Jews rather than blame the government for problems. They were determined to remain in the country where they had their homes and their livelihoods.

Many Jewish people, however, decided to leave. Between 1880 and 1929, over 3.5 million Jewish people abandoned eastern Europe – 2.3 million from Russia alone. They embarked on long, hazardous journeys, mostly to the USA. A minority believed they could never live freely among non-Jews and needed their own Jewish state. This was the central idea of Zionism.

RIGHT *The Zionist leader, Theodor Herzl.*

THE PALESTINIANS – A QUIET PEASANT LIFE

In the nineteenth century, Palestine was a rather remote province of the Ottoman Empire. Most of its people were peasant farmers, and smaller numbers lived in towns. The vast majority were Palestinian Arabs, mostly Muslim and some Christian. A few inhabitants were Jewish; they spoke Arabic and lived in peace with their Palestinian neighbours. Life was relatively calm and slow in pace.

ABOVE *Palestinian reapers at work in the fields in the early twentieth century, using traditional farming methods.*

From the 1880s, tens of thousands of Jews made their way from eastern and central Europe to Palestine, fleeing persecution. They set up their own separate farming communities. The Palestinians saw them as foreigners, isolated from the existing inhabitants and unwilling to integrate into Arab society. They grew more anxious about the number of newcomers.

? EVENT IN QUESTION

Land sales to Jewish immigrants

As part of their strategy to take over the country, the Jewish settlers wanted to buy land in Palestine. There was no shortage of Arab landowners willing to sell. Most of the land sold was occupied by tenant farmers (renting the land), who were then evicted. Among the sellers were leaders of the Arab nationalist movement. Some sold land because they needed the money, others so they could invest the cash elsewhere. According to Israeli journalist and historian, Tom Segev, *'Arab landowners were not forced to sell. They co-operated with the Zionists against the national interest of their own people.'* They were *'patriots on the outside, traitors on the inside'.* Were the landowners betraying their people? Or were they simply pursuing their business interests, as was their individual right?

FOILED PLANS FOR INDEPENDENCE

In 1917, during the First World War (1914–18), Palestine was conquered by Britain. In 1920 the British were officially given a 'mandate' over the country, which meant they were to rule it until such a time as they believed the local people could take over the government for themselves. Initially, both Jews and Arabs saw the British army as an army of liberation. They wished for independence and assumed they would win it under British guidance. But it soon became clear that there was no plan for the Arabs to develop their own nation.

In the period after the First World War, a wave of Arab nationalism swept through the Middle East. In Egypt, Syria and Iraq, the people demanded independence from the European powers that ruled over them. In Palestine, a similar movement developed. But here, not only were the Palestinians pitted against their British rulers. There were also Jewish settlers to contend with. The Arabs felt that the British had betrayed them. This led to huge resentment and disappointment, which increased as time went on.

ABOVE *A Jewish farm-worker ploughing the fields in Palestine. Women worked in the fields just as men did.*

THE YISHUV

'This postcard is the last one I write as a European; today, in a few hours, I will become an Asian. I have absolutely no regrets for that nice, cultured label European.'

Yefim Gordin, an eighteen-year-old Zionist from Vilna, Poland, on his way to Palestine in 1926

Jewish people had already started to move to Palestine because of the pogroms in late nineteenth-century eastern Europe. Things got no better for the Jews in the early twentieth century. During the 1920s, political crisis and rising unemployment in Europe led many to emigrate, some to Palestine. Then Hitler came to power in Germany in 1933 and introduced vicious persecution of the Jewish people. Within two years, 150,000 Jews left Germany, Poland and central Europe for Palestine.

? WHAT IF...

Jewish refugees had been welcomed in the USA and UK?

The favoured destination for most Jewish people fleeing the nightmare of Nazi persecution was actually not Palestine. Between 1935 and 1943, about 2.5 million Jews left Germany and its neighbouring states. Some 75 per cent fled to Russia. Only 8.5 per cent travelled to Palestine. The USA, where millions of Jewish people had already settled, was the 'promised land' of choice. But since the Quota Act of 1924, the USA had placed strict limits on immigration.

Britain also tightly restricted the numbers of Jews that could seek refuge there. If those fleeing Nazism had been welcomed in Britain and the USA in greater numbers, probably even fewer would have gone to Palestine – and there might not have been conflict with the Arabs.

JEWISH LAND FOR JEWISH PEOPLE

The Jewish settlement in Palestine was called the Yishuv. It was highly organized and grew quickly. The Jewish National Fund, established at the turn of the twentieth century, helped to organize the purchase of land for the Jewish settlers.

A Jewish trade union, the Histadrut, was founded in 1920. Its leaders coined a slogan to guide the colony: 'Jewish land, Jewish labour, Jewish produce.' Thus, Jewish people worked their own land, served only their own community and bought only their own produce. Out of the Histadrut came the political leadership of the Yishuv. The Jewish community governed itself, gradually building the structure of the future Jewish state.

A vital part of the strategy was the development of the kibbutzim. These were farming communities where everyone shared all the work, decisions and income. The vision of freedom and equality offered by the kibbutzim was open to Jewish people alone.

'If I knew it was possible to save all the [Jewish] children of Germany by bringing them over to England, and only half of them by transferring them to *Eretz-Israel*, then I would opt for the second alternative. For we must weigh not only the life of these children but also the history of the people of Israel.'

David Ben-Gurion, Zionist leader, December 1938

ABOVE *Jewish civilians line up outside the Warsaw ghetto in 1942, before being sent by the Nazis to the death camps.*

THE HORROR OF THE HOLOCAUST

From 1939 to 1941, Hitler's Nazi government in Germany occupied most of Europe. In 1942, the Nazis planned to transport all the Jews in occupied Europe to camps in Poland, where they would be made to work until they died. The unfit would be killed. This barbaric plan led to the Holocaust, in which 6 million Jews were killed, along with other groups including homosexuals, disabled people, Gypsies and Communists. Many Jews had already escaped Europe. As their fate became increasingly clear, millions more grew desperate to leave. The countries not occupied by Germany barely lifted a finger, although some brave individuals did help the Jews. In 1943, at the height of the murder campaign, the USA accepted only 4,705 Jewish refugees.

For many Zionists, establishing the State of Israel was more important than saving Jewish lives in Europe; they campaigned for greater Jewish immigration. Around 20,000 people made the dangerous journey during wartime across the Mediterranean Sea to Palestine.

After the Second World War, many Jews returned to their towns and villages but tens of thousands had lost their homes. Some were allowed to go to the USA. In 1947, there were still about 300,000 Jewish people in Displaced Persons' camps. No country really wanted them. At this point the United Nations voted to allow the creation of an Israeli state.

? WHAT IF...

the Holocaust had not happened?

Between 1880 and 1929, nearly 4 million Jewish people emigrated from eastern Europe. About 120,000 of them went to Palestine. Without the Holocaust, would Jews have gone to Palestine in such large numbers? Would the international community have supported the creation of Israel if there had been somewhere else for the Jews to go?

On the other hand, the Zionist movement was very determined and there was already a successful settler community in Palestine. Without the Holocaust, might the Yishuv simply have taken a longer time to achieve its goals?

LEFT *Three Jewish Holocaust survivors irrigate an orange grove on Kibbutz Buchenwald. While imprisoned in Buchenwald concentration camp, they had vowed to found a home in Palestine if they were ever freed. Their farm, founded in 1948, was named in memory of the vow.*

CHAPTER 3

The British in Palestine

D uring the First World War, Britain was a major world power with global economic interests. Palestine lay in an area of enormous strategic importance, on the sea route to the vital British colonies of India, South-East Asia and East Africa. Oil was the essential fuel needed to keep the wheels of war turning; Palestine was close to the Persian (now Iranian) oil fields and next door to Egypt, where Britain was trying to control a nationalist movement. The weakened Ottoman Empire would soon collapse, leaving a power vacuum in Palestine.

TWO PEOPLES, ONE LAND

Into this situation stepped the Zionist movement. One of its main leaders, Chaim Weizmann, was keen to form an alliance with Britain to secure Palestine for the Jewish people. Some within the British government thought a Jewish state would be a useful ally, while others believed their links with Arab countries in the region were more important. British policy shifted back and forth between the two world wars, attempting to keep a balance between support for the Zionists and the Palestinians.

BELOW *A Zionist delegation arriving in Palestine in April 1918 to visit the headquarters of General Allenby, the leader of the British forces.*

LEFT *A British sentry stands guard in Jerusalem after an outbreak of violence between Arabs and Jews in Palestine in 1922.*

The Balfour Declaration, issued by British Foreign Minister Lord Arthur Balfour in 1917, declared that 'His Majesty's Government views with favour the establishment in Palestine of a national home for the Jewish people.' The Palestinian Arabs felt betrayed; the peoples of the old Ottoman Empire had been promised that they could decide their own destinies after the war. In 1920, the Allied powers agreed at the San Remo conference that two separate states of Syria and Lebanon would be formed, under French mandate (or rule). Iraq and Palestine were to come under British mandate.

Naturally, the Palestinian Arabs were opposed to large-scale Jewish immigration and the idea of a Jewish state. After anti-Jewish riots by Palestinians in 1920, British policy swung back a little in their favour. In 1922, Jewish immigration was limited. However the policy was soon reversed, as Britain wanted to maintain good relations with the Jews. The number of Jewish immigrants swelled.

? EVENT IN QUESTION

The Balfour Declaration: a milestone for the Jewish state?

The Balfour Declaration did not establish a Jewish state, but the mention of a 'national home' encouraged the Zionist movement. Following the Declaration, the pace of Jewish immigration to Palestine increased. On the other hand, British policy shifted over the following years, and, at times, Jewish immigration was limited. While significant, the Declaration did not make a Jewish state inevitable.

THE 1936–9 ARAB REVOLT

During the 1920s, Palestinians demanded the right to form an Arab nation. They were also angry about the increase in Jewish settlers. There were demonstrations opposing Jewish immigration.

These protests turned violent in August 1929; 133 Jews and 116 Arabs were killed. In Hebron, 60 Jews were killed, mostly from an old Jewish community that was not even Zionist. Many were saved by their Muslim neighbours. Britain said that it recognized Palestinian fears but continued to allow a steady increase in Jewish immigration.

STRIKE AND REVOLT

In 1936 Arab anger erupted and a General Strike was called. The Palestinian community refused to co-operate with the

British or the Zionists. The Palestinians demanded an end to Jewish immigration and land sales, and wanted government by the majority population. The strike failed after six months, and was followed by a revolt that lasted until 1939. Palestinians took to the hills and engaged in guerrilla warfare against the British. The British responded by demolishing Arab villages and executing captured guerrillas.

The Arab economy was paralysed by the strike; Jewish settlers took advantage of this to develop their own economy. More settlements were built, and new roads and ports constructed. The British military authorities employed Jewish people in police units to help them to control the Arab uprising. By 1939, when the revolt was finally crushed, the Zionist movement was in a stronger position than it had been before.

? PEOPLE IN QUESTION

Hajj Amin al-Husseini

In 1921, Hajj Amin al-Husseini (1897–1974) was appointed by the British as Mufti of Jerusalem, the leader of Palestinian society. He blamed the Jewish settlers, rather than the British Mandate, for all the problems.

Al-Husseini supported the Nazi regime in Germany. In March 1933 he said to the German consul (government representative) in Jerusalem: 'the Muslims inside and outside Palestine welcome the new regime of Germany and hope for the extension of the fascist anti-democratic, governmental system to other countries.'

When the Arab rebellion broke out, al-Husseini was removed from power and fled to Lebanon. In 1941 he went to Germany, where his job was to encourage Arab support for the Nazi war effort. This helped to make the Palestinians unpopular in British eyes. Did al-Husseini have the Palestinian cause at heart or was he merely looking after his own interests?

LEFT British troops search Arabs for weapons at Jaffa gate (leading to the Old City of Jerusalem), as part of their attempt to prevent further riots, 1938.

21

THE JEWISH REVOLT AND ZIONIST PRESSURE

Some Zionists believed Jews and Arabs could live together in Palestine, while others thought there should be a Jewish state for Jews alone. After the Arab riots of 1929, the argument for a Jewish state, achieved through military force, grew more popular. During the 1930s and 1940s, the Yishuv gained more land and strengthened its economy.

However, in 1938-9, on the brink of war, Britain decided it was important to keep the Arab countries on its side. In May 1939, Britain announced that an independent state for both Palestinians and Jews would be established within ten years. This infuriated the Arabs, who wanted an independent Arab state. In addition, Jewish immigration would be limited to no more than one-third of the population. This infuriated the Zionists, led by David Ben-Gurion.

TERROR TACTICS

Some Zionists opted to use terrorist methods, to push the British out of Palestine. One group, the Irgun, was led by Menachem Begin. The other, LEHI (the Stern Gang), was commanded by Yitzhak Shamir. They bombed British targets around the country. At first, the Irgun and LEHI were condemned by most of Yishuv society. However, after the Second World War, the Yishuv's army, the Haganah – and its commando unit, the Palmach – joined the struggle. In June 1946, the Irgun bombed the King David Hotel in Jerusalem, killing more than 80 Arabs, Jews and Britons. In the same month, the Palmach blew up 11 bridges in a single night.

LOBBYING THE USA

The USA became more powerful during the Second World War. Keen to extend its influence in the Middle East because of the oil-rich countries there, it wanted good relations with the Arab nations. There was intense lobbying by American Zionists. Now that evidence of the horror of the Holocaust was out in the open, surely the remaining Jews should be helped? In 1944, Congress reluctantly declared it would help the Jews to establish a state.

The British Mandate (1917–48)

Could the promises the British made to Arabs and Jews ever have made it possible to reach a solution that was satisfactory to both sides? Perhaps not. Yet, in the 1930s, the Opposition (a coalition of Palestinian groups opposed to al-Husseini) was prepared to negotiate with the Yishuv. For example, it accepted continued but limited Jewish immigration. And, within the Yishuv, some Jews argued that there should be a bi-national state for both Palestinians and Jews.

ABOVE *After the bomb blast in 1946, British troops dig through the debris of the King David Hotel in search of casualties. The hotel had been used as the British headquarters.*

CHAPTER 4

1948 – A New State

In 1947, the British rulers of Palestine threw up their hands in despair and decided to refer the conflict-ridden land to the United Nations (UN) to sort out. The UN suggested dividing Palestine into two states, one for the Jewish people and one for the Palestinians. This was called the partition plan. It granted 55 per cent of Palestine to the Jews although they represented only 37 per cent of the population and owned just 7 per cent of the land.

AMERICAN SUPPORT

Competition between the new superpowers, the USA and the USSR, was intensifying. This was the start of the Cold War, when the USA and the USSR battled to gain influence over as many regions as possible. The United States now swung behind the partition plan, deciding that a new state of Israel would be a most useful ally in the Middle East. A US-backed state would be a counterbalance to the Arab states, which were increasingly coming under Soviet influence.

US President Harry Truman campaigned vigorously for the new state and threatened to withdraw Marshall Aid from countries that did not agree. (Marshall Aid was vital assistance for rebuilding countries after the devastation of the Second World War.) In November 1947, the UN General Assembly approved the partition plan by 33 votes to 13. None of the Arab states had agreed to it. In Syria, Egypt, Lebanon and Iraq, thousands of demonstrators poured on to the streets to protest.

The partition plan was a significant victory for the Zionist movement. The Arabs were devastated and rejected the plan. Palestinian historian, W. Khalidi, noted: 'The Palestinians failed to see why they should be made to pay for the Holocaust.' They rejected the idea that they were morally obliged to sacrifice their land because of the Jews' suffering.

? WHAT IF...

the Arabs had accepted the UN plan?

It could be argued that the Arabs made a mistake by not accepting the UN plan. As Israeli and Arab historians, Ahron Bregman and Jihan el-Tahri, say: 'With the benefit of hindsight, it is obvious that the failure of the Arabs to accept the 1947 partition proposal was a colossal historical mistake.' If they had accepted, they could have had an independent state alongside Israel.

However, parts of the Zionist movement were determined to gain control of as much of Palestine as possible. Even if the Palestinians had accepted partition, their enemies might still have wanted to go further and fight for more of the land. There is no certainty that the Arabs would have had their own state if they had accepted the plan.

WAR

The UN partition resolution in November 1947 did not ease the tensions in Palestine. From the moment the partition plan was agreed, clashes between Arab and Jewish groups increased. The British forces gave up all responsibility for law and order and the country slipped into civil war. The Jewish forces aimed to secure control over the territory allotted to them by the UN, and take over land to link it with the 33 Jewish settlements that fell outside the proposed Jewish state. The Palestinians tried to disrupt this and prevent the partition plan from being implemented.

RIGHT *Horror-stricken Jewish families flee from an explosion in Jerusalem, in February 1948, in which 51 people were killed. Arab forces later claimed responsibility for the bombing.*

LOCKED IN CONFLICT

The Jewish forces were made up of the Haganah, with about 45,000 men and women, and around 3,000 fighters in the Irgun and LEHI. All men and women aged 17 to 25 were called up to serve too. The Arab force was made up of volunteers from Palestine and neighbouring countries. One section was led by Abd al-Qadir al-Husseini, a very able leader. Palestinian forces numbered some 25,000 to 30,000 men in total. At first the Arabs were successful, but from April 1948 the Jewish forces gained the upper hand. The Arab forces suffered from a lack of central control and co-ordination, and the death of al-Husseini that month was a disaster for them.

This was a vicious war, with atrocities on both sides. For example, in February 1948, 60 Jews were killed by a car bomb in Jerusalem. On 9 April, 110 Palestinian men, women and children in the village of Deir Yassin, near Jerusalem, were killed by Jewish forces. The British now withdrew from Palestine completely.

LEFT *The British flag is lowered by a Royal Marine in Haifa, northern Palestine, in July 1948, signifying the end of the British mandate.*

? EVENT IN QUESTION

Deir Yassin: straightforward battle or bloody massacre?

When Palestinians spotted Jewish fighters from LEHI and Irgun coming to attack Deir Yassin village, they began firing. Jewish fighters threw grenades into homes, killing many people. The Arab fighters held out until LEHI got reinforcements, and then they were overwhelmed. Palestinian Abu Tawfik Yassini and Meir Pail, a Jewish commander, both recall that many more civilians were murdered after the Arab resistance was over. Meir Pail said: *'I saw twenty to twenty-five men stood up by the wall of the quarry and shot.'*

The following day, the local Palestinian leadership asked the surviving villagers to exaggerate the horror of what had happened, to encourage the Arab countries to support them. The plan backfired and instead led to thousands of Palestinians fleeing their villages in terror.

THE WAR OF INDEPENDENCE 1948–9

On 14 May 1948 the leaders of the Yishuv gathered in the Tel Aviv Museum and Ben-Gurion declared the establishment of the State of Israel. The USA recognized the Jewish state that same night. At 5 a.m. the following morning, Ben-Gurion heard Egyptian bomber planes overhead as Arab countries launched an attack on the new state.

The invading armies consisted of about 23,500 troops from Egypt, Jordan, Syria, Lebanon and Iraq. Clearly, the number of Arabs in the countries surrounding Israel was far higher than the population of the small country under attack. But the Arabs used only a fraction of their potential resources.

ISRAELI DETERMINATION

For Israel, this was a war of independence. The whole country was mobilized. New immigrants and foreign volunteers joined in the fight. At the start, Israel had nearly 30,000 men and women

BELOW *David Ben-Gurion (right) and other Jewish leaders meet at Tel Aviv Museum to sign the declaration of independence for the new State of Israel.*

RIGHT *Despite a ceasefire in August 1948, these Arab Legion soldiers in Jerusalem continue to fight Jewish troops.*

committed to battle; by the end of 1948 this had risen to more than 96,000. Many of the new immigrants came from Europe. They found the hot, harsh summer hard to cope with but they were incredibly determined. Golda Meir (a minister in the Knesset, the Israeli parliament) led a fundraising mission to the USA to raise money for weapons, which greatly boosted Israeli forces.

ARAB FAILURE

The Arab forces did not co-ordinate their battle plans. Also, they were suspicious of each other. For example, they all believed that King Abdullah of Jordan was keener to take land than to destroy Israel – a belief borne out by subsequent events. They were ill-prepared and believed their enemy would be easily defeated. As Egyptian officer Mourad Ghaleb said, 'We thought that the Jews were not courageous … not fighters.'

The war lasted until March 1949. For Israel, it had a lasting effect. It had come soon after the terrible tragedy of the Holocaust, and had cost the young country about 1 per cent of its total population, an extremely high proportion.

? EVENT IN QUESTION

1948–9: A life or death struggle for Israel?

Most Israelis certainly thought Israel was fighting for its survival in this war. Historian Ahron Bregman says that in hindsight this was true only during the first three weeks. During this time, the Arabs had superior weapons and firepower. However, Israel soon acquired new weapons and increased arms production. Its forces were well trained and dedicated to their cause. Nevertheless, the war was extremely bloody and traumatic for Israel.

THE YEAR OF CATASTROPHE, 1948–9

'Allon [the commander of central command] repeated his question: "What is to be done with the [Arab] population [of Ramleh and Lydda]?" Ben-Gurion waved his hand in a gesture that said: "Drive them out!"'

This extract, written by military commander Yitzhak Rabin, was censored – cut out – from his published memoirs. Ramleh and Lydda were areas allocated to the Palestinians under the partition plan, yet 50,000 people were forced to leave. This pattern of driving out Arab inhabitants was repeated around the country.

RIGHT *An elderly couple being escorted to waiting trucks that will take them and other Palestinians away from their homes in the southern Palestinian village of Al-Faluja to Gaza, in March 1949.*

Following the war of 1948–9, Israel controlled far more of the land than had been agreed in the UN plan – 78 per cent rather than 55 per cent. About half of the proposed Palestinian state was incorporated into Israel, and the remainder was taken over by Jordan and Egypt. Jordan took over the West Bank, including East Jerusalem, and Egypt acquired the Gaza Strip. Israel took West Jerusalem. The city of Jerusalem, holy to Jews and Muslims, was now divided.

FLEEING AS REFUGEES

About 750,000 Palestinians became refugees in Gaza, the West Bank and the neighbouring Arab states of Jordan, Lebanon and Syria. These countries were poor and it was hard for them to absorb refugees. The United Nations Relief and Works Agency (UNRWA) was set up by the UN in 1949 to run the refugee camps. As it became clear that Israel would not allow the inhabitants of the camps to return to their homes, they were given permanent refugee status. The Palestinians suffered terrible feelings of loss and humiliation. They call the events of 1948 *al-Naqba* – 'the catastrophe'.

BELOW *Thousands of Palestinian refugees, mainly from the towns of Lydda and Ramleh, gather in the Ramallah area, August 1948. They are in dire need of food and medical supplies.*

? EVENT IN QUESTION

Palestinians: forced to flee?

Israeli historians Benny Morris, Avi Shlaim and Ilan Pappé have researched documents that were secret at the time to reveal how Palestinians came to leave their homes. Benny Morris notes that *'there was no systematic expulsion policy; it was never, as far as we know, discussed or decided upon at Cabinet or IDF [Israeli Defence Force] meetings.'*

However, military attacks were just one cause for Arabs to depart. There was a general breakdown in law and order and a lack of direction by Palestinian leaders. Arabs were scared of living under Jewish rule. They felt abandoned by the Arab world. All this was on top of rumours about massacres – and actual massacres – by Jewish forces. So, in many cases, Palestinians were not forced out of their homes at gunpoint, but other factors made them decide to leave anyway.

CHAPTER 5

Israel – A Beleaguered Country?

In the years following Israel's independence, Egyptian or Syrian fighters would repeatedly attack Israel, and Israeli forces would retaliate, killing many more Arabs in return.

THE BATTLE FOR THE SUEZ CANAL, 1956

In 1952, Gamal Abdel Nasser seized power in Egypt, overthrowing King Farouk. President Nasser wanted to strengthen the Egyptian nation. In 1955 he made an arms deal with Czechoslovakia to buy huge quantities of weapons. The following year, he nationalized the Suez Canal Company. Nasser promised he would compensate those with shares in the company – mostly France and Britain – and use the money to build the Aswan Dam. The French and British governments were angry about losing control over this international waterway.

RIGHT *Map showing the Suez Canal, Straits of Tiran, Egypt, Israel, Sinai Peninsula and the military movements of the Suez conflict in 1956.*

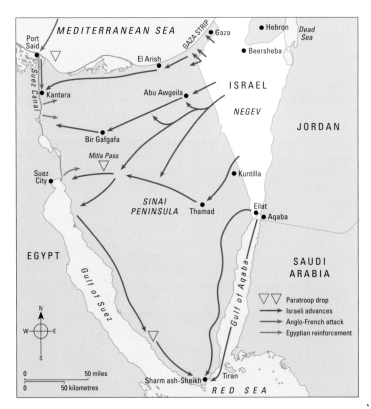

LEFT *The Suez conflict naturally increased Arab resentment of Israel. Here, Palestinian demonstrators in Gaza in 1957, just after the war, carry an effigy of Israeli Prime Minister David Ben-Gurion, wearing an Israeli flag.*

LIGHTNING WAR

France and Britain invited Israel to join them in a war to regain control of the Suez Canal. Israel was interested. Its leaders were worried by the quantity of weapons Egypt was acquiring and they wanted to gain access to the Straits of Tiran, the main trade route to East Africa and Asia. (Egypt did not allow Israel to use the Straits.)

On 29 October 1956, Israel attacked Egypt, occupied the Sinai Peninsula and opened the Straits of Tiran to Israeli shipping. Casualties on the Israeli side were minimal (172 killed and 700 wounded) while thousands of Egyptians died. But the Anglo-French force failed to conquer the Suez Canal.

After the war, the international community made Israel return the Egyptian territory it had occupied. The following few years were a period of relative peace between Israel and its Arab neighbours.

? PEOPLE IN QUESTION

Was Nasser a real threat to Israel?

The Israelis were convinced that Nasser was dedicated to attacking them, especially after the arms deal between Egypt and Czechoslovakia. Nasser certainly was building up his forces and presented a potential threat. Yet there is no evidence that he had an actual plan to attack.

Following the Suez war, Nasser became more resentful towards Israel, and his anti-Israeli declarations grew stronger. In 1958 he endorsed the anti-Semitic 'Protocols of the Elders of Zion', a fake document supposedly written by Jewish leaders planning the overthrow of the Western world. Five years later, he signed a communiqué (official statement), declaring '*The final account with Israel will be made within five years if we are patient.*' Nasser's threats were frightening for Israelis, but in reality it was they, heavily funded by the USA, who had the most powerful fighting forces in the region.

THE SIX-DAY WAR

The Six-Day War occurred partly because of superpower involvement in the region. It suited the USSR to create another trouble spot for the USA, already waging a war in Vietnam. The USSR also wanted the Arab forces to demonstrate that they were fighting with Soviet weapons and support.

SOVIET PROVOCATION

In May 1967, Soviet intelligence sources spread the false rumour that 'ten Israeli brigades had been concentrated on the Syrian border' ready to strike at Syria. Nasser, under pressure to defend his fellow Arabs, decided to close the Straits of Tiran. He knew this would provoke Israel into war. An uneasy few weeks followed. The USA did not want war, and the USSR now backed off, saying that it would not support Egypt. However, tensions had risen so high that war became unstoppable.

ISRAELI TRIUMPH

On 5 June 1967, the Israeli air force made a surprise attack on Egyptian planes. Within six days, Israeli forces had beaten the Egyptian, Syrian and Jordanian armies and occupied the West Bank, Gaza Strip, Sinai, the Golan Heights and East Jerusalem.

BELOW *Two Israeli tanks patrol East Jerusalem on 10 June 1967, five days into what became known as the Six-Day War. A very special Jewish holy site in Jerusalem, the Western Wall, came under Israeli control as a result of the war.*

This was a huge triumph for Israel, which now controlled 88,000 square kilometres of land (compared to 20,250 before the war). In addition, the entire holy city of Jerusalem was united under Israeli rule – a fact of enormous emotional, religious and symbolic importance.

This time Israel was not forced to return the conquered land. The USA continued to back Israel. Jewish settlements were established in the new territory. Groups of settlers built new communities, especially in the West Bank, to show that they wanted the occupation of the land to be permanent. Water supplies, a vital resource in this hot, dry region, were also seized. Palestinians fell under military rule. Many lost their land and livelihoods, and large numbers ended up working in low-paid, unskilled jobs in Israel. There was seething resentment of the Israeli occupation.

Areas occupied by Israel during the 1967 war
Cease-fire lines, 10 June 1967

0   50 miles
0   50 kilometres

ABOVE *Map showing territories occupied by Israel during the 1967 war.*

? EVENT IN QUESTION

The 1967 occupation: benefit for Israel or millstone around its neck?

In some ways, having control of more territory gave Israel increased security. The conquered areas formed a buffer (safety) zone around the centres of population, making it harder for Arab states to attack Israeli citizens. The establishment of Jewish settlements allowed the country to absorb more immigrants. Natural resources were exploited too.

But there were also dangers. Israel now occupied land where 1.3 million Palestinians lived. They most definitely did not want to be under Israeli rule. The occupation led to divisions within Israeli society. Many believed the land should be returned to the Arab countries in exchange for guarantees of peace, while some felt that the whole area of historic Palestine should remain in Jewish hands for ever.

THE YOM KIPPUR WAR

In the war of October 1973, Egypt and Syria attempted to take back the territories lost in 1967. Egypt wanted to regain the Sinai Peninsula, Syria and the Golan Heights. And a victory against Israel would restore wounded Arab pride.

ABOVE Egyptian troops, elated at having crossed the Suez Canal during the Yom Kippur War. However, around 12,000 Egyptian soldiers were killed in the war; Israel lost about 2,300 dead.

A COUNTRY AT PRAYER

The Arab armies attacked Israel on the holiest day of the Jewish calendar, Yom Kippur, completely taking the country by surprise. At first, the Egyptian forces were successful, crossing the Suez Canal into Israeli-occupied Sinai. Feeling confident, they moved deeper into the Sinai than had been planned and over-extended themselves. This made it easier for the Israeli forces to fight back. The Israelis soon gained the initiative in the Golan Heights too; after a week, the Syrian forces were on the defensive.

ISRAEL HITS BACK

Ten days into the war, with the help of sophisticated weapons obtained from the USA, the Israelis managed to destroy Egyptian anti-aircraft guns so that their jets could fly over Egypt. On 16 October, General Ariel Sharon recalled, he 'heard a field commander's voice come over the radio saying: "We can get to Cairo! [Egypt's capital]".' At this point the United Nations called for a ceasefire. The USA put pressure on the Israeli Prime Minister, Golda Meir, not to go further into Egypt because of the risk of the USSR becoming involved on the Arab side.

The President of Egypt, Anwar Sadat, had lost the war but had crossed the Suez Canal and won an important battle against Israel. For the first time, Egyptian and Israeli representatives negotiated peace terms directly. In Sadat's mind was the desire to reach a lasting peace with Israel and just four years later (see pages 52–53) he was to astonish the world.

? PEOPLE IN QUESTION

Was Golda Meir responsible for Israel's lack of readiness?

The Yom Kippur War was a huge shock for the Israelis. Once the guns fell silent, the government began to investigate who was responsible for Israel being caught unawares. The Agranat Commission looked into the events and put much of the blame on the military, rather than on Meir and Defence Minister Moshe Dayan. However, there was huge public pressure on the government over the issue, and in April 1974 Meir resigned. She did not join the new government. It would probably be true to say that several people, both military and political leaders, were responsible. But Meir was Prime Minister and her reputation was damaged by the failure to predict war.

ABOVE *Golda Meir, before she became Prime Minister, posing with children on a kibbutz.*

37

LEBANON – AIDING THE ENEMY'S ENEMY

Israel's northern neighbour, Lebanon, used to be known for its beautiful mountains and lively capital, Beirut. But from 1975 the country endured civil war. Christian forces fought the Muslims and Palestinians. Many Palestinian refugees lived in Lebanon, and the Palestine Liberation Organization (PLO), led by Yasser Arafat, was based there. From Lebanon, PLO fighters made occasional raids on northern Israel, endangering communities there. Israel retaliated against these raids.

In 1976, the Lebanese government invited Syrian forces to try to stop the civil war. That year, Israel secretly started to back the Christian forces. The PLO was an enemy shared by the Israelis and the Lebanese Christians, and the Israelis did not want Syria to take over Lebanon. Israel launched its own military operation against the PLO in Lebanon in March 1978.

SHARON AT THE HELM

BELOW Israeli soldiers crouch behind a wall as they conduct searches for Palestinian guerrillas in fierce house-to-house fighting in Lebanon in 1982.

In 1981 Ariel Sharon became Defence Minister. Ben-Gurion once said of him: 'He's a brilliant soldier, but a vicious man'; many Israelis shared this view. Sharon was determined to rid Lebanon of the PLO once and for all. The following June, he launched an invasion of Lebanon. The USA, Israel's superpower backer, disagreed with it, but neither stopped nor condemned the attack. The Israeli

army laid siege to West Beirut, where the Palestinians and Muslim Lebanese lived. The Lebanese pleaded with Arafat to make the PLO leave – and they did.

In August 1982, Bashir Gemayel, leader of the Lebanese Christians, was elected President. He was assassinated the following month. On the same day, Israelis allowed Christian forces to go into the Palestinian refugee camps of Sabra and Shatilla, supposedly to pursue Palestinian fighters. The Christian troops were eager to avenge Gemayel's death – although Gemayel had in fact been murdered by a Syrian. The militia massacred somewhere between 700 and 2,000 Palestinians in cold blood, shocking the entire world.

ABOVE *A Palestinian woman weeps over the bodies of her relatives in the Palestinian refugee camp of Sabra in West Beirut, Lebanon, 1982. In the background, a Red Cross volunteer is spraying disinfectant.*

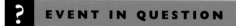

? EVENT IN QUESTION

Sabra and Shatilla: Israel's responsibility?

Official Israeli statements said that Israeli troops were not present when the massacres occurred but this has been shown to be untrue. One Israeli battalion commander sent this message to his men about the killings: *'We know, it's not to our liking, and don't interfere'.*

There is no evidence that Israeli soldiers took part in the killing of Palestinians in Sabra and Shatilla. It could be argued that Israel was not responsible because it only gave the Christian militia permission to pursue fighters – not murder entire families of refugees. Nevertheless, Israel was allied with the Christian militia. Surely its forces could have stopped the massacre if they had wanted to?

THE 1991 GULF WAR

In August 1990, President Saddam Hussein of Iraq shocked the world when his forces occupied neighbouring Kuwait. He hoped to take over Kuwait's vast oil supplies and sell the oil to rebuild his country, bankrupt after its long war with Iran (1980-88).

The USA was worried that Saddam Hussein, whose regime it had long supported, was becoming unduly aggressive. Perhaps Iraq would go on to invade oil-rich Saudi Arabia too? Most Arab states and Western countries condemned the invasion of Kuwait. A UN resolution was passed, calling for Iraq to withdraw from Kuwait.

A CLEVER LINK

BELOW *As they withdrew from Kuwait, Iraqi troops set fire to the Kuwaiti oil wells. Here, an American fire-fighter tries to extinguish a burning well in the Al-Ahmadi oil fields in south Kuwait, June 1991.*

Saddam Hussein then made a cunning move. He proposed that there should be solutions to all the occupations in the Middle East, including the Israeli occupation of Palestinian, Syrian and Lebanese territory. This proved extremely popular with ordinary Arabs across the region. US President George Bush realized that, unless he promised negotiations towards a settlement of the Arab-Israeli conflict, he would have difficulty building a coalition against Saddam Hussein. In October 1990, he announced that there would be a conference to resolve the conflict, following Iraq's withdrawal from Kuwait.

WAR ON IRAQ

Saddam Hussein refused to go willingly. In January 1991, a US-led military coalition, including some Arab forces, attacked Iraq. Saddam Hussein now launched Scud missiles against Israel, a hated enemy, causing fear and panic there. He hoped that Israel would retaliate so that the Arab countries would withdraw from the war against him. They would not want to be on the same side as Israel.

The USA persuaded Israel that it would be against its interests to retaliate. Bush called Israeli Prime Minister Yitzhak Shamir, and said: 'Prime Minister, you really can't do this, you'll be playing into the hands of your number one enemy.' By the end of February 1991, Iraq had been defeated. President Bush knew it was time to restart the Arab-Israeli peace process.

? WHAT IF…

Israel had retaliated against Iraq?

Israel might well have retaliated against the missile attacks by Iraq. Within the Israeli cabinet, some ministers were in favour of action. Unsurprisingly, Ariel Sharon thought that Israel should attack, using its air force to bomb the missile sites in western Iraq, and even taking ground forces through Jordan if necessary. If Israel had attacked Iraq, it would have created serious problems for the coalition against Saddam Hussein, which included many Arab countries. They would have been under intense pressure from their citizens to support Iraq against Israel and the coalition might have fallen apart.

ABOVE *Two Iraqi girls walk past the remains of a building in the capital, Baghdad. It has been destroyed in bombing by the US-led coalition forces during the first Gulf War, 1991.*

CHAPTER 6

The Story of the Palestinians

Mrs Zamzam: 'The men stayed behind but we left the next day. I held my son Hassan who was 40 days old and the small children carried the other babies. We took the keys to the house with us – we lost them here in Rashidiyeh.' In 1948, when Jewish forces shelled her village in northern Palestine, Mrs Zamzam and her children fled to Lebanon. And there they remained.

BELOW *Marka Camp, 10 km east of Amman, Jordan, houses over 20,000 Palestinian refugees. Many of the older generation fled in 1948, when Israel was established, and others arrived after the 1967 war.*

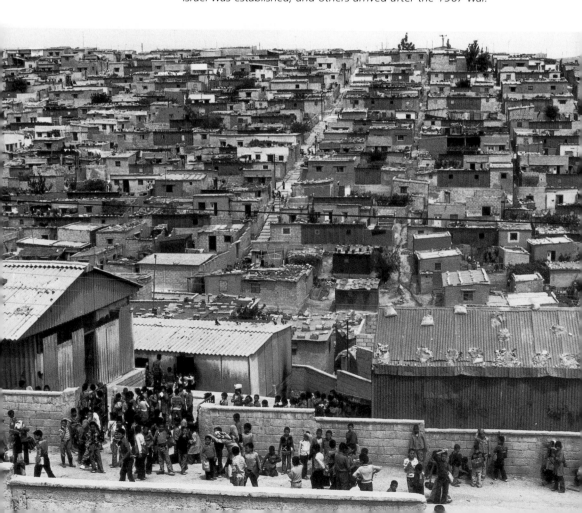

PERMANENT REFUGEES

During the war of 1947–9, about 750,000 Palestinians fled or were forced out of their homes in the new state of Israel. They resettled in the West Bank and Gaza Strip, and in Jordan, Syria and Lebanon. A few moved to other Arab states, or to countries where they had connections, such as the UK or the USA.

According to Israeli historian, Benny Morris, 'The war's end found less than half of the Palestinians in their original homes.' The majority had left most of their possessions behind, in the belief that they would soon return. Now they had nothing, and had no choice but to live in refugee camps. To help these stateless people, the United Nations set up the United Nations Relief and Works Agency (UNRWA) in 1949.

Following the Six-Day War in 1967 and the Israeli occupation of the West Bank, Gaza Strip and East Jerusalem, a further 200,000–300,000 Palestinians fled or were driven from their homes, mostly going to Jordan. Another 80,000–90,000 left the Golan Heights. Around 14,000 were allowed back in after the war but the rest remained refugees.

RIGHT *Palestinian refugee students in Gaza start a new school year in 2002. Their school is run by UNRWA.*

? EVENT IN QUESTION

The establishment of UNRWA, 1949

Today UNRWA provides health, education and social services to 3.9 million Palestinian refugees in Jordan, Lebanon, Syria, the West Bank and the Gaza Strip. One-third of them live in refugee camps in poor conditions, *'with a high population density, cramped living conditions and inadequate basic infrastructure such as roads and sewers.'* (UNRWA, 2003). The remainder live around the camps or in other parts of the host countries.

UNRWA was set up as a temporary measure. It has retained responsibility for refugees to this day because there has been no solution to the Arab-Israeli conflict. It could be argued that, if it had not been established, the surrounding Arab countries would have had to take responsibility for the refugees and integrate them into their communities. However, most refugees have never wanted this; they still demand the right to return to their land. UNRWA's existence has always reminded the world that the situation has not been resolved.

THE PALESTINE LIBERATION ORGANIZATION

Those Palestinian refugees who had money or a profession managed to make a reasonable life for themselves in other Arab lands. Meanwhile, for the 80 per cent of registered refugees described by UNRWA as peasants, unskilled workers and their families, life was tough. It was hard to find work. In Arab states they were treated worse than workers from the host country. The refugees felt humiliated. By the early 1960s, they realized that they could not rely on the Arab nations to win back Palestine for them. The watchword became 'self-reliance'.

THE RAPID GROWTH OF FATAH

Fatah, meaning 'victory', became the largest of several guerrilla organizations that recruited young volunteers to join an armed struggle to regain their land. In 1964, President Nasser of Egypt and the other Arab leaders formed the Palestine Liberation Organization (PLO) to try to control the new movement and ensure that it did not upset Arab states. Yet it grew rapidly and could not be controlled. In 1965, Fatah launched its first attack on Israel.

After the Six-Day War (see page 34) in 1967, there were angry protests in the newly occupied territories. These protests were rapidly suppressed by Israel, increasing Palestinian resentment and leading to further armed resistance against the occupation. In 1968, for example, the Palestinians fought the Israeli army at Karameh, Jordan.

FREEDOM FIGHTERS OR TERRORISTS?

The guerrillas believed they were 'freedom fighters' and that it was necessary to use violence to free their land. They thought nobody would listen to them otherwise. Their opponents saw them as terrorists, ruining lives and causing terrible devastation. How effective were their tactics? They certainly got themselves known for their actions – by 1970, the whole world had heard of the Palestinians. At the same time, the violent tactics undermined sympathy for their cause.

? EVENT IN QUESTION

The Battle of Karameh

In March 1968, Israeli forces attacked the village of Karameh in Jordan in response to the blowing up of an Israeli school bus by Palestinian guerrillas. The Jordanians and the PLO guerrillas put up far more resistance than the Israeli army had expected. They became heroes throughout the Arab world.

Yet this may have led to their downfall in Jordan. The PLO became a liability for the Jordanian government, causing instability. Indeed, two years later, King Hussein crushed the PLO. On the other hand, Palestinian historian, Edward Said, said that the Battle of Karameh divided Palestinian history into 'before', when the Palestinians relied on other Arabs, and 'after', when they fought back for themselves.

LEFT *An Israeli soldier places an explosive charge at an ammunition dump at Karameh, Jordan, in March 1968. The Israelis believed that the ammunition store was being used by Fatah guerrillas.*

45

A CAMPAIGN OF TERROR

Between 1968 and 1970, the PLO grew strong in Jordan. King Hussein became concerned that the Palestinians, who formed two-thirds of the Jordanian population, would overthrow him.

Members of Fatah, the main group in the PLO, did not believe in challenging Arab regimes. They wanted other Arab countries to help them win back Palestine. However, smaller groups – such as the Popular Front for the Liberation of Palestine (PFLP) and the Democratic Front for the Liberation of Palestine (DFLP) – had Communist ideas. They wanted to topple Arab regimes, fight Israel and bring about a Palestinian revolution.

HIJACKING, HOSTAGES AND KIDNAPPING

In September 1970, the PFLP hijacked three Western aeroplanes, taking hostages. The hijackers released most of the hostages and blew up the planes in Jordan. King Hussein felt he was losing control of his kingdom. He launched a full-scale assault

BELOW *The Munich apartment where two Israeli Olympic team members were murdered by Palestinian guerrillas in September 1972. Nine others were taken hostage and later also killed by their captors.*

King Hussein: betrayer of the Palestinians?

King Hussein was in a difficult position. A large proportion of his population was Palestinian, yet the Palestinian struggle threatened his reign. The PFLP and DFLP wanted to overthrow him and use Jordan as a base from which to regain Palestine. By 1970, law and order was breaking down in Jordan; there was even an attempt on the king's life. King Hussein recalled when the hijackers blew up three planes: *'Well, that was the limit. As far as I was concerned, something had to be done – and done quickly.'* He gave the order to attack the PLO. For the Palestinians, this was a complete betrayal by an Arab leader but for King Hussein the survival of his rule was at stake.

on the PLO camps and bases and pushed out the Palestinian guerrillas. This expulsion became known as Black September.

The Palestinians saw that the Arab states would support them to a certain point but would not accept a challenge to their rule. A new desperation set in. Palestinian guerrillas resorted to spectacular acts of terrorism that created enormous publicity combined with huge disgust at their tactics. They hijacked planes, massacred passengers at airport check-in counters, and blew up individual Israelis. In 1972 one group kidnapped Israeli athletes at the Munich Olympics, murdering them all before they were overcome by the German police.

In the years following Black September in 1970, most Palestinian guerrillas escaped to Lebanon. The existence of a PLO base in Lebanon added to the tensions there (see page 38). In 1982, after the Israeli invasion, the Lebanese also expelled the PLO and Yasser Arafat was sent away to Tunisia.

ABOVE *King Hussein of Jordan, seen here leaving the capital, Amman, in September 1970.*

INTIFADA

After Israel took control of the West Bank and Gaza Strip in
1967 (see pages 34–35), Jewish settlements were established on
Palestinian land, making it clear that the occupation was there
to stay. By 1988, as much as 55 per cent of the land in the West
Bank and 30 per cent of Gaza was in Israeli hands.

In the 1970s, the Israeli administration tried to set up political institutions in the Occupied Territories to work with Israel
and control the Palestinians. This did not succeed. The majority of the Palestinians remained nationalists, determined to win
back their land. Resistance continued and was severely pun-
ished. At the end of 1987, the intifada (uprising) erupted.

NO LONGER AFRAID

Masses of unarmed protesters – men, women and children –
surged on to the streets throughout the West Bank and Gaza
Strip, throwing stones at Israeli soldiers armed with guns and
tanks. General strikes and a boycott of Israeli goods followed.
The Palestinians developed a new self-confidence: 'No one is
afraid of their [the Israelis'] guns any more,' protesters in Gaza
told journalists.

To stop the intifada, Israel tried shooting to injure or kill,
beatings, mass arrests and imprisonment without trial.

According to Israeli human rights organization, Be'tselem, between December 1987 and the end of 1992, Israel's security forces killed 956 Palestinians in the Occupied Territories and Israel. During the same period, 78 Israeli civilians were killed by Palestinians.

The intifada forced Israel and the world community to stop ignoring the Palestinians. The Palestinians could not get the Israelis out of the Occupied Territories and Israel could not stop the violence. Both sides realized they needed help to end the conflict. The uprising only ended with the Oslo peace agreement of 1993 (see page 54).

BELOW *These young Palestinian demonstrators have been caught by Israeli military police after rioting, in Ramallah, West Bank, March 1988.*

? PEOPLE IN QUESTION

Yitzhak Rabin's 'breaking bones' policy: unnecessary cruelty or cruel necessity?

Yitzhak Rabin, Israel's Defence Minister during the intifada, had a hard task. The Israel Defence Forces (IDF) were used to warfare against foreign armies or guerrillas but had little experience of mass civil unrest. In 1988, Rabin introduced a policy allowing soldiers to use clubs against demonstrators. He let slip in a TV interview that the intention was to 'break [rioters'] bones'.

In Rabin's favour, the 'beatings policy' did put off the rioters for a while, and caused fewer deaths than shooting. Yet it made the Arabs hate Israel even more. People around the world saw images of Israeli soldiers cruelly beating Palestinians. Israelis could be viewed as the bullies and Palestinians as the victims.

ABOVE *An Israeli security guard holds his hand over Ariel Sharon's face to protect him from rocks being thrown by Palestinians during his visit to the Temple Mount on 28 September 2000.*

THE AL-AQSA INTIFADA

By 2000, the Palestinians lived under the rule of a local Palestinian Authority, although Israel still had overall military control of the Occupied Territories. The Camp David talks of 2000 had failed (see page 56), leaving frustration and tension on both sides. In September, Israeli right-wing opposition leader Ariel Sharon decided to visit the Temple Mount in Jerusalem, an area holy to Muslims as well as to Jews. A number of mosques, including Al-Aqsa, are situated there. Sharon's visit was intended to demonstrate Israel's rights over the city of Jerusalem. He knew it would provoke the Palestinians.

This was the spark that ignited a new intifada. Riots spread throughout the Occupied Territories; Arab-Israelis (Palestinians living in Israel) protested too. Horrendous violence on both sides followed. The death of a twelve-year-old Palestinian boy, caught on camera, led to frenzied attacks on Israelis. In Ramallah, West Bank, two Israeli soldiers were lynched by a mob. Their bodies were displayed on TV, causing outrage in Israel.

A CYCLE OF VIOLENCE

This time the Palestinians had guns, hand grenades and mortars, not just stones. They struck at Jewish settlers, as well as the Israeli security forces. The Israelis felt justified in unleashing their full might against them, using fighter jets, helicopter gunships and tanks. An assassination policy was introduced, to kill Palestinians who were leading the violent attacks on Israelis. Of particular concern were leaders of the militant movements, Hamas, Islamic Jihad and the Al-Aqsa Brigades. These organizations were completely opposed to the peace process, and were murdering Israeli civilians in suicide bombing missions.

The Palestinians had become increasingly desperate. In 2003, despite a measure of local rule, they remained under military occupation with no freedom of movement. Israel continued to take their land to build Jewish settlements. Unsurprisingly, a minority had turned to violent means to try to put pressure on Israel.

RIGHT *Female suicide bomber Andaleeb Taqatqa, aged 20, in an amateur video released by an armed group linked to Fatah. Taqatqa blew herself up near an outdoor market in Jerusalem in 2002, killing six people and injuring 89.*

? PEOPLE IN QUESTION

Ariel Sharon: tough leader or brutal bully?

Ariel Sharon, who was Defence Minister during the invasion of Lebanon in 1982 (see page 38), believed that the use of military force was the only way to stop Palestinian violence. In March 2001, a few months after the start of the Al-Aqsa intifada, he became Israeli Prime Minister. His supporters felt only a tough leader like Sharon could control the security situation. But, to the Palestinians and many Israelis, he was a brutal bully who used military force to deal with a political problem – the Palestinians' desire for their own state. They believed this policy was doomed to failure.

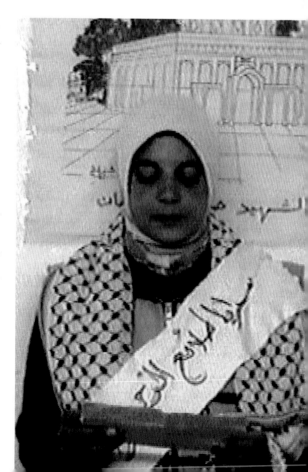

The Peace Process

Throughout the years of conflict between Israel and the Arab states, there have been attempts to make peace. After the wars of 1947–9, 1956, 1967 and 1973, the Arab states realized that Israel was a force to be reckoned with. To varying degrees, Israel's neighbours grudgingly began to accept its existence.

Anwar el-Sadat became President of Egypt in 1970, following the death of Nasser. Sadat planned to rely less on the Soviet Union and to develop closer ties with the USA. He even wanted to seek genuine peace with Egypt's greatest enemy, and the USA's closest ally in the Middle East – Israel.

BELOW *Israeli Prime Minister, Menachem Begin (centre), with President Sadat of Egypt (left) during Sadat's visit to Israel in 1977.*

AN ARAB LEADER IN JERUSALEM

In November 1977, Sadat surprised the world by becoming the first Arab leader to visit Israel. Nervous Israeli officials thought the visit might be a trap – perhaps Sadat's plane was full of terrorists who would leap out of the aircraft and

kill the Israeli leaders waiting at the airport! Sadat spoke in the Knesset, the Israeli parliament, declaring 'I come to you today on solid ground to shape a new life and establish peace.'

However, the actual peace negotiations were harder work than the speeches and grand gestures. In summer 1978, US President Jimmy Carter acted as go-between at the Camp David talks in the USA, soothing tensions between Sadat and Israeli Prime Minister, Menachem Begin. It was agreed that Israel would give back the Sinai to Egypt although it would retain control of the West Bank and Gaza Strip. A peace agreement was eventually signed in March 1979.

Sadat's move, while celebrated in the West, was deeply unpopular in the Arab world. In 1981 Sadat was assassinated by Muslim extremists. He had paid for peace with his life.

? PEOPLE IN QUESTION

Anwar el-Sadat: inspired or misguided?

On the one hand, it was extremely courageous of Sadat to negotiate directly with Israel. It was also good for Israel, enabling the country to develop diplomatic and trade links with an Arab country, and to use the Suez Canal for shipping. War between Israel and the Arab countries became less likely because Egypt, the strongest country, was out of the fight.

However, Sadat went to Camp David arguing that Israel should return all the Arab land it occupied in 1967 and allow the Palestinians to form their own state. Israel refused to give up control of the land and Sadat accepted this. Was he misguided to leave the question of the Palestinians to fester?

CONDITIONS FOR COMPROMISE

In 1988, the PLO declared it would accept a 'two-state solution' – a state of Israel and a state of Palestine – rather than attempting to regain the whole of Palestine. Following that, the break-up of the Soviet Union between 1989 and 1991 meant less backing for the Arab states. This made it harder for them to take on Israel in military conflict, so they were more willing to negotiate. Furthermore, one of the outcomes of the Gulf War of 1991 was a commitment to resolve the Arab-Israeli conflict. Israel was also under pressure (from the intifada) to compromise with the Palestinians.

THE OSLO ACCORDS

In 1991, talks between the Arab states, the Palestinians and Israel were held in Madrid, Spain. Many months of secret meetings between Israelis and PLO members then took place – such contact was illegal for Israelis. Finally, in August 1993, the Oslo Accords were agreed. A temporary self-governing Palestinian Authority was to be set up for five years, leading to a permanent settlement. Within three years, negotiations would begin over Jerusalem, the Palestinian refugees, Jewish settlements and security. In September, the agreement was signed at the White House in Washington DC, USA.

During negotiations over the following three years, the Israelis withdrew their forces from Gaza and from many West Bank cities and villages. In 1996, Palestinian elections were held and Yasser Arafat won a landslide victory. A Palestinian Authority ruled the Palestinians for the first time. Yet Israel still possessed 60 per cent of the West Bank and 40 per cent of the Gaza Strip, and had overall control over the land, security and water supplies.

BELOW *An Israeli flag and a white dove of peace fly over a rally of more than 250,000 people in November 1995. They are paying their last respects to Prime Minister Yitzhak Rabin, assassinated the previous week.*

? PEOPLE IN QUESTION

Yitzhak Rabin: man of peace or man of war?

Under Prime Minister Yitzhak Rabin, peace agreements were signed with the Palestinians and a peace treaty with Jordan was concluded in 1994. Rabin received a Nobel Peace Prize in 1994. But he was attacked both by extreme Islamic groups and by Israeli right-wingers, neither of whom could tolerate compromise. Following a pro-peace rally in Tel Aviv, Israel, in November 1995, a lone Israeli gunman fired at Rabin. The Prime Minister died shortly afterwards. Many supporters of Rabin felt that the peace process would have continued to progress if he had not been assassinated.

But Palestinians did not agree that Rabin genuinely wanted peace with them. He was the man who had led the Israeli forces against the Arabs during the Six-Day War and used brutal tactics against them during the intifada.

ABOVE *An Israeli flag flies in front of a new housing block under construction at a settlement east of Jerusalem, in May 2001.*

A LONG PROCESS, WITH LITTLE PEACE

Following the assassination of Rabin, there were further attempts to make peace between Israel and its Arab neighbours. A final Israeli withdrawal from Lebanon was secured in 2000. Yet successive Israeli prime ministers, Benjamin Netanyahu and Ehud Barak, were unable to agree with the Palestinians over the thorny issues left undecided by the Oslo Accords.

DEADLOCK AT CAMP DAVID

At the Camp David talks in 2000, US President Clinton proposed that Israel hand over 94–96 per cent of the West Bank to the Palestinians, close most Jewish settlements, and allow some Palestinian refugees back to the West Bank and Gaza Strip. A division of Jerusalem was proposed. This sounded generous, but the Palestinians argued that even if Israel held on to just a small portion of the land, its army would still be able to control them. The Palestinians did not agree that Israel should maintain overall military rule over the West Bank and Gaza Strip. Neither did they accept that refugees should give up the principle of the right to return. President Clinton publicly praised Barak and blamed Arafat for the deadlock.

A CONTINUED CYCLE OF VIOLENCE

The Palestinians' frustration with the situation led to the Al-Aqsa intifada in September 2000 (see page 50). Ariel Sharon was elected Prime Minister of

Israel the following February. He firmly believed that the uprising had to be crushed by force before a peace agreement could be attempted. As opinion on both sides hardened, the conflict intensified.

There were more suicide bombings in Israel, leading to more invasions of Palestinian towns and refugee camps by the Israeli army, and the killing and maiming of civilians. Meanwhile, new Jewish settlements, roads for settlers, and military bases continued to be built in the Occupied Territories.

BELOW *Palestinian Authority security policemen arrest a member of Hamas at his home in the West Bank city of Hebron, in December 2001, following a series of suicide attacks inside Israel.*

? PEOPLE IN QUESTION

Yasser Arafat: could he stop terrorism?

Powerful forces within Palestinian society did not accept compromise with Israel. Two main groups, Hamas and Islamic Jihad, believed in trying to win back the whole of Palestine for the Muslims. They were prepared to kill Israeli security forces and civilians to put pressure on Israel to give back their land.

The Israeli government expected Yasser Arafat, the head of the Palestinian Authority, to control the Palestinians and they provided weapons for his police force. Arafat did indeed imprison many Islamic militants. But others soon replaced them. With sufficient will and force, could Arafat have crushed their movement? Or could it be argued that, while the political problem of Israeli control remained, resistance – including terrorism – was also likely to continue?

Is Peace Possible?

'In the early 1950s Ben-Gurion believed that peace with the Arabs would eventually dawn, but only after Israel hit them over the head again and again, until they were persuaded that Israel was too resolute and too strong to beat.'

Benny Morris, Israeli historian

Was Ben-Gurion right? Following victory in several wars, Israel has indeed signed peace accords with Egypt and Jordan, although not with Syria and Lebanon. Nevertheless, other Middle Eastern countries, such as Iraq, Iran, Libya and the Gulf States, remain opposed to Israel.

What Do Israelis and Palestinians Want?

The Israelis want safety from terrorist attack and secure borders. Most would prefer the Palestinians to live separately, whether in their own state or under Israeli rule. Some would rather the Palestinians were 'transferred' to other lands altogether. A minority of Israelis support the Palestinians, for example, by protesting about the building of Jewish settlements on occupied land, and promoting dialogue.

Most Palestinians want their own independent state that they can control. Many accept that this state will lie side by side with Israel and that they will never regain all of what was Palestine. They would like the right to return to their land, even though most refugees would not actually come back. And they want control over their holy places in Jerusalem.

A Road Map to Peace?

Following the US-led war in Iraq in 2003, the USA made a commitment to kick-start the peace process with a 'road map' for a solution. But the Palestinians feel that the key player – the USA – still favours Israel. Since its birth, Israel has received one-third of all aid given by the US each year. The USA has never forced Israel to make concessions to the Palestinians although they have accepted the State of Israel on 78 per cent of former Palestine. Whether Israel and the Palestinians can agree on a compromise and end the conflict remains to be seen.

EVENT IN QUESTION

Building the separation barrier

From 2002, a 350-km wall was being built between the West Bank and Israel, as a defence against terrorist attacks by Palestinians. The aim was to physically keep out the Palestinians. To enable it to be built, 36 Palestinian villages lost farmland, and 32 towns and villages were cut off from other West Bank communities. Crossing points were heavily guarded by Israeli security forces, which controlled movement between the two sides.

The wall may reduce attacks in the short term. Yet the restriction of movement has already increased resentment among the Palestinians. Without a political solution to the conflict, can building a wall stop terrorist incidents?

BELOW *Mahmoud Abbas (left), who was appointed Palestinian Prime Minister in April 2003, with Israeli Prime Minister Ariel Sharon (right) and US President George W. Bush (centre). However, Abbas was unable to progress the peace process and resigned his post just four months later.*

Timeline

1914–18
The First World War.

1917
Britain conquers Palestine.
NOVEMBER: The Balfour
Declaration is made, a British
statement of support for a
national home for the Jewish
people in Palestine.

1920
The Histradrut, a Jewish trade
union, is founded in Palestine.
Palestinian riots against Jewish
settlers.
APRIL: San Remo conference
gives France a mandate to rule
Syria and Lebanon, and
Britain a mandate to rule Iraq
and Palestine.

1921
Hajj Amin al-Husseini is
appointed Mufti of Jerusalem.

1924
The US Quota Act imposes
strict limits on immigration to
the USA.

1929
Arab-Jewish conflict in
Palestine causes deaths on
both sides.

1933
Adolf Hitler comes to power
in Germany.

1936
Arab General Strike in
Palestine.

1936–9
Arab revolt in Palestine.

1939–45
The Second World War.

1939
MAY: Britain announces that
an independent state for
Palestinians and Jews will be
formed within ten years.

1942
The Nazis plan to murder all
the Jews in Europe, leading to
the Holocaust.

1944
The US Congress declares
that it will help the Jews to
form a state in Palestine.

1946
The Irgun bombs the King
David Hotel in Jerusalem.

1947
The UN approves a partition
plan for Palestine, dividing it
into a Jewish state and a
Palestinian state.

1947–8
Civil war in Palestine.

1948
APRIL: Murder of villagers of
Deir Yassin by Jewish forces.
MAY: The establishment of
the State of Israel.

1948–9
War between Israel and the
Arab states.
Palestinians flee or are forced
out of their homes in Israeli-
occupied land.

1949
UNRWA is set up to assist
Palestinian refugees.

1952
Gamal Abdel Nasser takes
power in Egypt.

1956
Nasser nationalizes
the Suez Canal.
OCTOBER: Israel makes a
successful attack on Egypt and
as a result gains access to the
Straits of Tiran.

1964
The PLO is formed.

1967
The Six-Day War: Israel
defeats Egypt, Syria and
Jordan.

1968
The PLO and the Jordanians
fight the Israelis at Karameh,
Jordan.

1970

The PFLP hijacks three planes and blows them up in Jordan.
Anwar el-Sadat becomes President of Egypt.

1972

Palestinian guerrillas kidnap and kill Israeli athletes at the Munich Olympics.

1973

Yom Kippur War: Egypt and Syria attack Israel to try to take back territory lost to Israel but are beaten.

1974

Israeli Prime Minister Golda Meir resigns.

1975

Civil war in Lebanon begins.

1976

Syrian forces move into Lebanon.
Israel starts to back the Christan forces in Lebanon.

1977

President Sadat of Egypt visits Israel.

1978

Israel launches Operation Litani against Lebanon and establishes a Christian-dominated 'security zone' inside Lebanon.

1979

A peace agreement between Egypt and Israel is signed.

1981

President Sadat of Egypt is assassinated.

1982

Israeli Defence Minister Ariel Sharon launches an invasion of Lebanon.
AUGUST: The PLO leaves Lebanon.
SEPTEMBER: Christian forces murder Palestinians in the refugee camps of Sabra and Shatilla, Lebanon.

1987

The intifada in the Occupied Territories begins.

1988

The PLO says it will accept a State of Palestine alongside the State of Israel.

1990

Iraqi forces occupy Kuwait.

1991

The USA leads the first Gulf War against Iraq.
Talks between Israelis and Palestinians in Madrid, Spain.

1993

The Oslo Accords are signed by Israel and the Palestinians.

1994

A peace treaty between Israel and Jordan is signed.

1995

Israeli Prime Minister Yitzhak Rabin is assassinated.

1996

Yasser Arafat wins the Palestinian elections.

2000

Camp David talks between Israel and the Palestinians.
SEPTEMBER: The outbreak of the Al-Aqsa intifada.

2001

Ariel Sharon is elected Prime Minister of Israel.

2002

APRIL: Sharon orders Operation Defensive Wall, an attack on Palestinian cities aimed at stopping terrorism against Israelis.
Building of a wall to separate the West Bank from Israel begins.

2003

The USA leads the second Gulf War against Iraq.
APRIL: The USA presents a 'road map' for peace, outlining the creation of a Palestinian state alongside Israel.

Glossary

anti-Semitism Hatred of Jewish people, which by the late nineteenth century had become a new kind of hatred based on ideas about 'racial difference'.

bi-national state A state for two peoples to share, in this case the Israelis and the Palestinians.

British Mandate The British Government's authority to run another country.

coalition A group formed by people of different political parties or countries, agreeing to work together for a particular political purpose.

commando unit A group of soldiers trained to make quick attacks on enemy areas.

Communist A person who follows Communism as in the former Soviet Union, believing that the state should control the production of goods on behalf of the people.

curfew An order for people to stay in their homes for a certain period of time.

Democratic Front for the Liberation of Palestine (DFLP) A Palestinian political organization, formed in 1968, with the aim of winning back Palestine through armed struggle and revolution.

Displaced Persons' camps Refugee camps set up after the Second World War for people who had no homes to go back to.

General Strike A strike of workers in all the most important areas of the economy.

guerrilla warfare Fighting by small groups of soldiers who are not part of a regular army, against a regular army.

Haganah The main military organization of the Jewish settlers in Palestine, 1920 to 1948.

Hamas A militant Palestinian Islamic organization, formed in 1987 in the West Bank and Gaza Strip, which aims to create an Islamic state in Palestine.

intifada Palestinian uprising against Israeli occupation; used to describe the uprisings that began in 1987 and 2000.

Irgun A Jewish right-wing underground movement, formed in 1931, which called for the use of force to establish a Jewish state.

Islamic Jihad An Islamic organization in the West Bank and Gaza Strip that became influential from the mid-1980s, especially in Gaza. It argues for 'holy war' against Israel and liberation of what was Palestine.

Islamic state A state that is run according to the laws of Islam alone.

Knesset Israeli parliament, in Jerusalem.

LEHI (Stern Gang) Zionist terrorist organization, formed in 1940. It attacked British targets in its aim to win a Jewish state.

lobby To meet or attempt to influence (someone with political power) in order to persuade them to support one's beliefs.

lynch As a group, to capture someone considered guilty of a crime, and kill them.

memoirs An account written by somebody famous about their life and experiences.

militant Willing to use force or strong pressure to achieve political or social change.

militia A group of people who are not professional soldiers but who have had military training and can act as an army.

mortar Heavy gun for firing shells into the air.

nationalism The desire of a group of people who share the same culture and language to form an independent country; also pride in one's country.

nationalize To put an industry or company under the ownership and control of the government.

Nobel Peace Prize A prize that is awarded each year to a person or people who it is considered have made the biggest contribution to world peace.

Occupied Territories The Palestinian land occupied by Israel after the 1967 war: the West Bank, Gaza Strip and East Jerusalem.

Ottoman Empire An empire that at its peak included all of Asia Minor and much of south-eastern Europe. It lasted from the thirteenth century until the establishment of Turkey in 1922.

Palestinian Arab/Palestinian An Arab born in what was Palestine, or born to a family that comes from Palestine.

Palestinian Authority Palestinian government within the Occupied Territories that was established

Further information

under the Oslo Accords of 1993.

Palestine Liberation Organization (PLO) An organization formed in 1964 to co-ordinate various Palestinian resistance groups, and to struggle for the creation of a Palestinian state.

persecution Treating someone in a cruel and unfair way, e.g. because of the person's race, culture, religion or political beliefs.

pogrom Organized killing of large numbers of people, especially because of race or religion.

Popular Front for the Liberation of Palestine (PFLP) A Palestinian political organization, formed in 1967, with the aim of toppling Arab regimes through armed struggle, destroying Israel and creating a Palestinian revolution.

Protocols of the Elders of Zion A fake document, first published in Russia in 1903, which was used to promote anti-Semitism. It was claimed that the document was written by Jewish leaders who were planning the overthrow of the Western world.

Quota Act A law allowing only a certain number of people – a quota – to immigrate to a country each year.

refugee A person forced to leave their country because of war or for political, religious or social reasons.

Scud missile A long-range guided missile, fired from one point on the ground or in the sea to another.

security forces The forces that protect a country, such as the police and the army.

suicide bombing When a person wearing explosives strapped to the body goes to a crowded area and deliberately blows him or herself up, along with the surrounding people.

superpower A country that has very great military or economic power and a great deal of influence.

United Nations (UN) An international organization with almost all the world's states as members.

Yishuv Jewish settler community in Palestine up until the State of Israel was formed.

Zionism Political movement that aimed to establish an independent Jewish state. Now concerned with support and development of Israel.

BOOKS

Virginia Brackett et al, *Menachem Begin* (Chelsea House Publications, 2002)

Anna Claybourne, *Golda Meir* (Heinemann Library, 2003)

David Downing, *Yasser Arafat* (Heinemann Library, 2002)

Nathaniel Harris, *New Perspectives: Israel and the Arab Nations in Conflict* (Hodder Wayland, 1998)

Michael Kort, *Yitzhak Rabin: Israel's Soldier Statesman* (Millbrook Press, 1996)

Ivan Minnis, *Troubled World: The Arab-Israeli Conflict* (Heinemann, 2001)

Oxfam, *Making Peace: Oxfam Educational Handbook* (Oxfam Educational, 1996)

Colleen Williams, *Yasir Arafat* (Chelsea House Publications, 2002)

NOTE ON SOURCES

A source is information about the past. Sources can take many forms, from books, films and documents to physical objects and sound recordings.

There are two types of source, primary and secondary. Primary sources date from around the time you are studying; secondary sources, such as books like this, have been produced since that time. In general, primary sources are more accurate but contain much narrower information than secondary sources.

Here are some guidelines to bear in mind when approaching a written or drawn primary source:
1. Who produced it (a politician, cartoonist, etc?) and why? What was their motive? Were they trying to make a point?
2. When exactly was the source produced? What was going on at the time?
3. Might the source have been altered by an editor, censor, translator?
4. Where was the source produced? Which country, town, region, etc?
5. Does the source tie in with other sources you have met, primary and secondary, or does it offer a new point of view?
6. Where has the source come from?

Index